The Group Reunion

THE  LIBRARY

The Group Reunion

Stephen D. Bryant

UPPER ROOM BOOKS
NASHVILLE

THE GROUP REUNION
Copyright © 1996 by The Upper Room®
All rights reserved.

No part of this book may be used or reproduced in any manner whatsoever without written permission of the publisher except in the case of brief quotations embodied in critical articles or reviews. For information, write Upper Room Books®, 1908 Grand Avenue, Nashville, Tennessee 37212.

The Upper Room® Web site http://www.upperroom.org

UPPER ROOM®, UPPER ROOM BOOKS® and design logos are trademarks owned by the Upper Room®, Nashville, Tennessee. All rights reserved.

Scripture quotations not otherwise identified are from the New Revised Standard Version of the Bible, copyright © 1989 by the Division of Christian Education, National Council of the Churches of Christ in the United States of America. Used by permission.

Cover design: Jim Bateman
Third printing: 2000

Printed in the United States of America

Stephen D. Bryant, a past International Director of the Walk to Emmaus® movement, is currently Editor/Publisher, The Upper Room®.

Contents

What Is an Emmaus Group Reunion? 7

How Do I Join a Group? 10

How Do We Start? 13

What Do We do from Week to Week? 17

How Can We Encourage Congregational
Group Reunions? 24

How Can We Enhance Our Group
Reunion's Effectiveness? 29

Resources 37

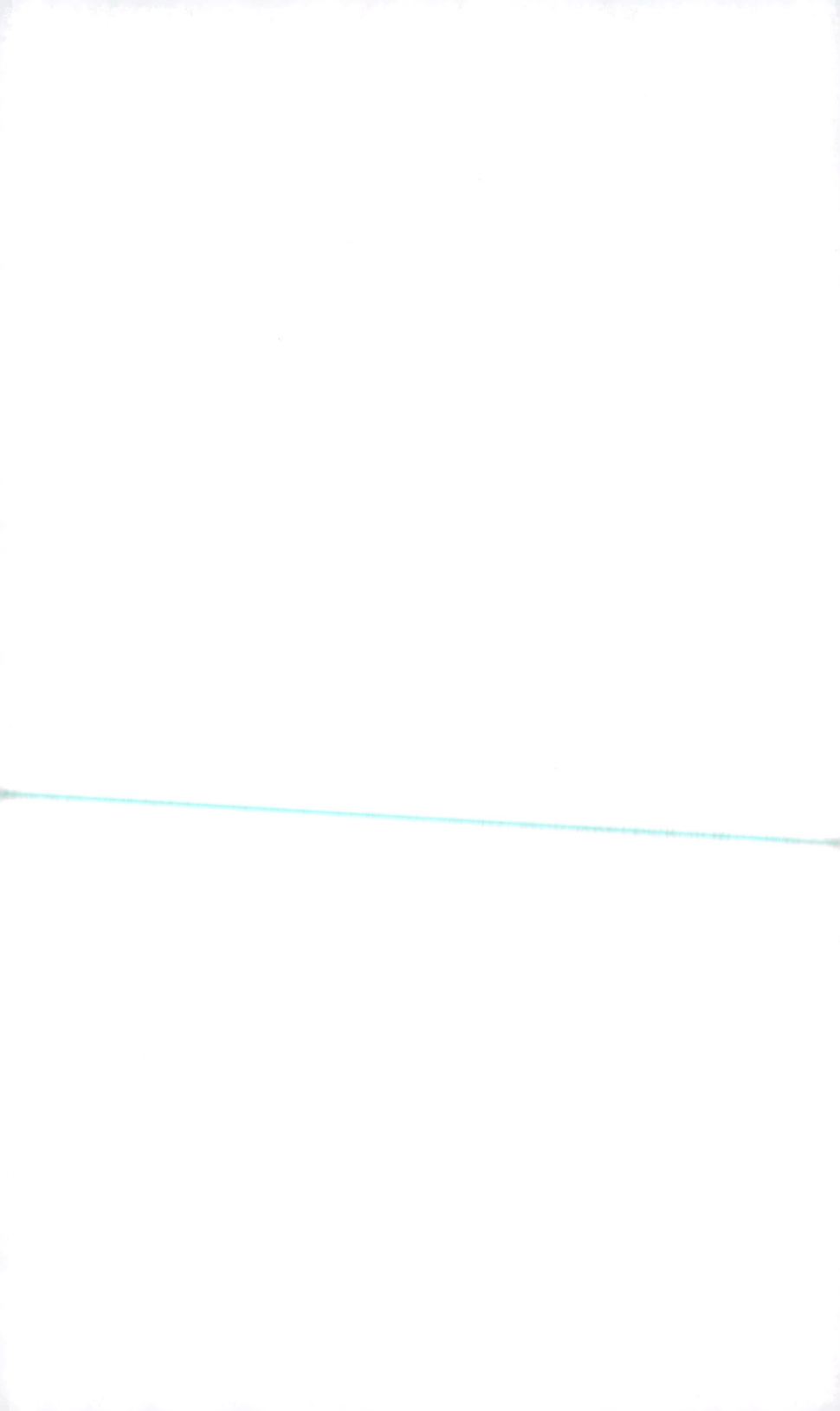

What Is an Emmaus Group Reunion?

he Emmaus group reunion is a small accountability group of two to six persons who have usually participated in the three-day Walk to Emmaus and who want to continue their pursuit of a life lived wholly in the grace of God. These small follow-up groups help pilgrims translate the message conveyed on the Walk to Emmaus weekend into a daily walk with Christ. With the regular support of a few faithful friends, the gift of God's love in Jesus Christ becomes a lifestyle of Christian discipleship through the threefold discipline of piety, study, and action.

Perseverance in Grace

Persons may call their group reunions by different names: "reunion groups," "fourth day groups," "accountability groups," "share groups," "discipleship groups," "journey groups," and "Christian support groups." Irrespective of name, group reunions have a common purpose: to help us persevere in grace. Group reunions undergird our desire to carry those aspects of the three-day experience that we most value and that are fundamental to our formation as faithful Christian disciples into our everyday lives.

How do we persevere in grace? The talk on Perseverance tells us that the key is regular contact with Christ and with other Christians who share the vision of life lived wholly in the grace of God. The group reunion then becomes a dynamic means of support and maintenance of meaningful contact with Christ and other Christian friends for the long haul. The spiritual companionship of the group reunion encourages us in our practice of the means of grace—the ways Christ instructed and modeled for us to stay in touch with him, to share his life and mind, and to grow in his love and likeness.

Reviewing Our Daily Walk

Group reunions meet at regular times, usually weekly for an hour. The meeting consists of persons' sharing the stories of their walk with Christ during the past week. A pattern provided on the group reunion card, which everybody receives on the third day of their Emmaus weekend, guides the sharing:

① Each person reviews the manner in which he sought to walk with Christ through the threefold discipline of piety, study, and action.
② Each person reflects on the ways she experienced Christ's walking with her in holy moments and in calls to service.
③ Each person shares plans for living out his or her discipleship in the week to come.

The meeting concludes with announcements and closing prayers.

Members listen to one another, celebrate the grace of God in each person's life, and reinforce each one's core commitment to living in union with Christ in all facets of daily life. Members express that reinforcement through gentle accountability, encouragement, and support of one's stated discipline and plans.

Varieties of Groups

Men and women commonly form separate groups. This separation is partly an outgrowth of friendships made in separate men's and women's Emmaus weekends. Persons may feel that groups of mixed gender inhibit their personal sharing. But many groups form without regard to gender. Some people prefer groups that include men and women. Still others enjoy the advantages of meeting as married couples. Most groups are all laity, some include clergy, and a few are all clergy.

The Presence of the Holy Spirit

Emmaus groups that effectively support Christian growth do not come about by our human effort alone. We certainly do our part: we get together, practice our discipline, and go to the meetings. But it is the Holy Spirit who opens our hearts to God and to one another, who makes us spiritual friends, who weaves us together and prompts us with ways to watch over one another in love. The Holy Spirit connects us with others like ourselves who are ready for such a group and whose gifts will blend. For this reason, forming groups requires earnest prayer and openness to God's little surprises. Sometimes the last persons we would have chosen for our groups show up there and turn out to be the best for us. And sometimes the first persons we would have chosen simply do not work out. ✞

How Do I Join a Group?

wo routes are available for joining a group. Either you may seek out a group that is already in process or you may seek out friends to form a new group. Joining a group requires personal initiative and prayer. While persons are ready to assist you, no one will automatically match you with a group. Group reunions represent a step of faith on the part of people who are taking personal responsibility for their lives as Christians with the help of the Holy Spirit.

Friendship Networks

Emmaus groups form most naturally among friends or among persons who already have some basis of relationship, such as the Emmaus experience, membership in the same church, or simply a common desire to be more intentional about one's Christian discipleship. Each of these is a solid foundation for building an accountability group:

- *Friends in your church.* Look for persons in your church who have been to Emmaus or who already show a desire to live as intentional Christians. If church members who have been to Emmaus have not already contacted you about being in a group reunion, then contact them. Emmaus groups deepen the spiritual bonds within congregations. They focus attention on the basics of Christian discipleship. And they enable members to connect with others in the fellowship who want to push out into deeper spiritual waters. You also might consider joining other kinds of accountable discipleship groups within the church.
- *Friends in the Emmaus community.* Look for persons in the local Emmaus community with whom you would feel comfortable sharing. Go to the follow-up meeting after your Walk to

Emmaus weekend. Review the list of pilgrims on your Walk, especially your table friends. Make friends within the Emmaus community by attending monthly gatherings or by volunteering to work in the kitchen on future Walks. Make known your desire to join a group. Seek out the Follow-up Chairperson and ask for assistance in locating groups that may need additional persons or in locating individuals who might want to create a new group.

✞ ***Colleagues at work.*** Sometimes groups form among persons who work together, not only for the convenience of meeting but for missional purposes. These "environmental group reunions," as persons sometimes call them, try to pay special attention to the manner in which they live out their faith in the workplace. The groups become a base for being the church in the workplace, for approaching one's work with the mind of Christ, and for reaching out to others in that setting who feel called to more intentional Christian discipleship.

Successful groups often form among persons who do not really know one another but who build new friendships based on their common desire to live as accountable Christians. Some persons actually prefer the freedom they experience when meeting with persons they do not relate to in other contexts.

Schedules

Often the logistics of a particular group determine its membership—who can meet when and where. Some churches and Emmaus communities have gatherings designed to enable individuals to find others who can meet at the same preferred time during the week.

Expected Group Changes

Expect some change in the membership of group reunions. Members move away, secure new jobs, get married, have babies, transfer churches, alter schedules, undergo crisis, and change as persons. The combination of external factors that make some groups possible may change, making the same groups impossible a few years down the road.

Change also occurs when groups deliberately reach out to help ensure that every person who goes through Emmaus will have a group to join. Before inviting a new person in, give group members a chance to talk about the addition and to agree. Groups must live with the tension between the call to remain open to new persons and the value of preserving a stability that members may now enjoy. Bringing in new members is always an act of faith and a sacrifice of love.

Sometimes persons may change groups for personal reasons—to start new groups, to join a group with persons who share similar goals or needs, to get a fresh start apart from difficult past relationships. No one needs to feel obligated to stay in the same group forever.

Available Assistance

When you are having trouble joining a group, pray that the Spirit open your eyes to potential companions among the people around you. Call on those persons who can offer assistance: your sponsor, your table leader from your Emmaus weekend, the Follow-up Chairperson in the Emmaus community, and your pastor or other church staff. ✟

How Do We Start?

hoose a suitable time and place to meet. Settle on a meeting time that is acceptable to everyone—early mornings before work, over lunch, after work, in the evenings, Saturday mornings, or Sunday afternoons. Your group may have to get together several times before you determine a convenient meeting time. Find a location that is both convenient and conducive to your purpose. Some groups meet in churches and homes. Some groups meet in restaurants or offices. Two important factors are these:

① Enough time for everyone to share.
② A place that provides some protection from interruption. Choose a place that allows members to share personally and to pray together without feeling inhibited or distracted by acquaintances or waiters.

Keep the Group Small

For a group of two to six persons, one hour is sufficient time for each person to share and for relationships to develop. Beyond six members, an hour's time frame severely limits each person's sharing, and closeness within the group becomes increasingly unrealistic. Larger groups would do well to form two or three smaller groups that meet at various times, thereby enabling more persons to participate actively in groups.

When the members of a large group strongly desire to stay together, consider gathering as a whole for the opening prayer, then forming several small groups of three to five persons to work through the service sheet, the questions on the card, and a moment of prayer for one another. Come back together as a whole for the last few minutes to share Emmaus group activities, prayers for special needs, and the closing prayer of thanksgiving.

This approach preserves both the small-group intimacy and the camaraderie of the larger gathering. Married couples have used this same approach effectively by forming a group of men and a group of women after the opening prayer.

Review Purpose and Agenda

When you meet to organize as a group, make sure everyone's expectations are consistent with the purpose and design of group meeting. As long as individuals want to live a whole life in grace through a lifestyle of piety, study, and action—then the group reunion format will prove effective in providing reinforcement and accountability. But if what the members really want is more particular—a Bible study, a prayer group, an outreach, or a group counseling situation—then the group reunion format will not serve their needs. This lack of clarity about group purpose is a common cause of some groups' lack of success.

Clarify Commitment to God

When you join a group reunion, you are renewing your response to God's love and committing to love God in return through a lifestyle of piety, study, and action. But what do "piety, study, and action" really mean until translated into specific patterns of behaviors?

The area of piety, for example, includes such things as worship, communion, meditation and prayer, spiritual direction, and retreat. But as a rule, through which of these avenues will you give God your attention? When and for how long? Study and action must be more than occasional bursts of inspiration. The point is to develop daily, weekly, and monthly patterns for reshaping your life as a walk with Christ. The goal is a lifestyle of living in grace.

Take some time alone to decide upon the actual shape of your baseline offering to God in the areas of piety, study, and action. For example, "As a rule, my piety will include worship on Sundays and daily prayer for fifteen minutes. My study includes preparation for the church school class I attend. My action includes monthly service at the family shelter. I meet weekly with my group. In addition to this, I remain responsive to the promptings of the Holy Spirit to love God and neighbor in all that I do." Start the journey with little steps that are specific and doable rather than setting ambitious goals that may end in discouragement.

Clarify Commitment to One Another

Your relationships with one another will grow and change as you journey together by faith. But the group members need an initial covenant with one another to define the circle of commitment within which the group reunion can effectively sustain the perseverance and growth of its members. We may define that circle of commitment by at least these four characteristics: seriousness, sincerity, discretion, and regular attendance.

Seriousness does not mean heaviness and humorless exchange. It means bringing to the meeting a single-mindedness with respect to the real business of the group reunion and the vision of a life in grace. Without a degree of seriousness, the group will be unable to support anyone's movement forward. Persons display seriousness in their punctuality, in their pursuit of relevant and worthwhile conversation, and in their earnestness about practicing personal discipline during the week.

Sincerity means presenting yourself to one another in a spirit of honesty, genuineness, and openness. It means being real. An atmosphere of unconditional acceptance among members fosters sincerity. Sincerity manifests itself in nonjudgmental attitudes, simplicity of speech where persons speak only for themselves, and loving attentiveness to Christ in the others.

Discretion is the discipline of holding what members share in confidence. When members handle their knowledge of one another with care and prayer, trust can grow. This trust can foster depth, intimacy, and true support for one another in times of struggle. Discretion also shows up in the caution with which members reveal to the group, even for the purpose of prayer, details about the struggles of people who are not group members.

Regular attendance is the most obvious and elemental aspect of the shared covenant. The commitment to attend is both for yourself and for one another. Attendance is your weekly re-affirmation of the form of life toward which you seek to grow. It is also a weekly affirmation of your commitment to the spiritual welfare of your friends. The times when you least want to attend will be those when another member needs the group most. At the outset, agree on a time and a place for meeting that maximizes the possibility of everyone's regular attendance. ✞

What Do We Do from Week to Week?

ach person who attends the Walk to Emmaus receives a group reunion card on the third day. The outline of the card reflects the flow of the weekly meeting.

Prayer to the Holy Spirit

The group begins the meeting by reciting the prayer on the card. The "Prayer to the Holy Spirit" is a centuries-old prayer paraphrase of Psalm 104:30, which celebrates God's sovereignty over humanity and the Spirit's recreative work in this world. The opening prayer is a reminder that the reason for meeting is not only to be with one another; it is to gather with openness to the renewing presence of the Holy Spirit. The prayer signifies the group members' recognition that the Spirit accompanies them in their daily walk and in their weekly gathering, just as the spirit of Jesus accompanied the two disciples on the walk to Emmaus that first Easter afternoon.

Service Sheet

The service sheet represents a basic outline of each person's service to God in the areas of piety, study, and action. After the opening prayer, each member of the group reviews the service sheet. Each member shares what he or she did in each of these areas for the sake of being present to God during the week. The review is more meaningful when made in view of specific commitments. For example, "My usual practice is solitary prayer each morning before leaving for work, but I was only successful in keeping my discipline four of the days because . . ." or "I got so involved in my study time that my usual one hour of study on Sunday nights turned into two hours!"

By sharing the benefits as well as the difficulties encountered in the keeping of the discipline, the review becomes more than a legalistic ticking off of pious practices. The time becomes a rich opportunity to gain insight into one's life patterns, areas of resistance, and learnings about the walk of faith.

Closest Moment to Christ

After everybody has reviewed the quality of their service and presence to God during the past week, the group moves on to the reflective questions. The attention shifts to their awareness of Christ's presence and call to them in the midst of everyday life. The first question is, "At what moment this past week did you feel closest to Christ?"

The Emmaus road story illustrates the meaning of the question. Grief, disappointment, and loss of faith dominated the two disciples' experience of life. And yet, in the midst of their anguish, the risen Christ "drew near and went with them." God's love broke through to them even in their desolation. And so, we ask ourselves each week —if not each day—what situations and challenges have dominated our experience of life? In what ways has Christ drawn near in the midst of it all, and where have we known God's love?

We may experience Christ's closeness in a moving worship service, in an act of compassion, in a time of joy and gratitude, or in a sense of assurance about a tough decision. Avoid limiting awareness of Christ to only positive experiences. What about Jacob's closeness with God when he wrestled with God through the night? (See Genesis 32:22-32.) What about Mary's troubling experience when visited by the angel Gabriel? (See Luke 1:26-38.) Whether for comfort or challenge, close encounters with Christ always open us to Christ's redemptive presence afresh. They are reaffirmations of God's love and faithfulness.

Call to Discipleship

"At what moment during this week did you feel you were responding to God's call to be a disciple? Where did you participate in being the Church this week?"

The message of the Walk to Emmaus is that God loves each of us with an unconditional love and that our discipleship consists in sharing that gift of love with others. In reviewing the service sheet, we share how we followed through on our planned commitments to Christian action. In the "Call to Discipleship" we examine our awareness and responsiveness to God's call of love in the midst of everyday life. When did we help someone become open to God's love? When did we reach out to a friend in need or go out of our way for someone we did not even know?

The question invites us, first of all, to think positively about the ways we responded faithfully to God's call to love, witness, and service during the past week. Responsiveness to God's call of love often comes naturally. When Jesus came as a stranger to the two disciples on the road to Emmaus, they received him without question into their company. When they arrived at Emmaus, they invited him to stay over and to share their food.

By naming even those ways in which our discipleship comes naturally, we celebrate the ways in which God's grace is active already in who we are. Discipleship is seldom a rare and heroic deed. It is, at its best, a lifestyle of grace that expresses itself in everything we do.

The question also challenges us to reflect upon the ways God may be beckoning us to share Christ's love in new and unanticipated ways. Which persons continually surface in prayer and thought? What human need continues to interrupt our peace? What injustice keeps us awake at night? Sometimes faithful response requires planning and collaboration with others. Sometimes it means changing our plans. Sometimes it means sacrifice. Sometimes it means finally forgiving someone or seeking forgiveness in a relationship that needs healing.

Discipleship Denied

"When was your faith tested this week through failure?"

This question has two sides. First, the question invites us to review ways in which our best efforts as disciples were denied, obstructed, or rendered fruitless during the past week. For example, the crucifixion of Jesus clearly reflected the world's denial of Jesus' and the disciples' ministry. Apparent failure tested their faith. But what did God accomplish through, or in spite of, their failure? What did they learn about following Jesus and about the walk of faith?

Jesus' journey with his disciples makes it clear that the experience of failure is inherent in the call to discipleship. We find our faith tested when persons reject our efforts at reconciliation, take advantage of our attempts at generosity, do not return our investments of love and energy, and disregard our attempts to witness.

Only those who never try to follow Jesus avoid failure. And yet, the potential in these experiences is to grow in grace through adversity. God uses failure when we give it over in faith. Christ teaches us the meaning of the call to faithfulness, not success. We learn to surrender the fruit of our actions to God.

Another side of the question of discipleship denied is the naming of the ways in which we failed to be responsive to God's call to love and service during the past week. Like Peter, we stood by warming ourselves at the fire while truth was being crucified. (See Luke 18:25.) Like the rich young ruler, we were unable to respond to love's call with the necessary commitment. The aim is not to beat up on ourselves but to become aware of our "no" to God and resistances to grace that are still active in all of our lives. We acknowledge the ways in which Christ's perfect love does not yet reign in our lives. We identify opportunities for further growth in the love and likeness of Jesus Christ.

Your Plan

"What is your plan for piety, study, and action for the week to come?"

Living as a Christian disciple requires planning. Disciples are not spiritual wanderers but pilgrims on an intentional journey with Christ. Our spiritual growth is not accidental but is the result of purposeful participation in the means of grace. For this reason, members of the group develop plans. The general framework for their plan is piety, study, and action—three all-encompassing dimensions of Christian discipleship.

At this time, each member of the group updates his or her commitments for the coming week in the areas of piety, study, and action. Based on the past week's experience, a person may improve a particular approach to prayer or adjust his or her devotional time to be more realistic. The focus of study might change from scripture to a social need. This week's experience of an unanticipated call to discipleship may lead to new commitment to an action plan for the upcoming week.

By making plans, we can discern movement on the path of discipleship. By sharing plans for the upcoming week, we make ourselves accountable. By remembering others' plans, members strengthen one another's resolve to follow through on commitments.

Reunion Group Activities

Reunion groups provide a natural launching pad for mission in the community. Reunion groups are also a support base for acts of agape for Emmaus weekends. Shared engagement in service to others deepens friendships and opens up avenues for Christian action.

Some groups, where members relate to the same church, find a shared ministry within their congregations. Other groups choose to serve together in the kitchen for an Emmaus weekend or make it their mission to set up facilities for Emmaus weekends. Many groups spend time making table agape, creating banners, and writing general agape letters to support their own and other Walks to Emmaus. Some Emmaus groups take on ministries in their local communities.

As valuable as group activities and a sense of common mission can be, Emmaus groups must remember that these efforts are "extracurricular." Always make time for the primary work of the group —reviewing the service sheet and reflecting on Christ's presence and call.

Prayers for Special Needs

Shared prayer is an important means of growing together in love and of kindling the fires of God's love for the days ahead. Before closing, the group takes a few minutes to lift one another to God in prayer, giving special attention to needs, circumstances, and decisions that surface during the meeting. Members voice special prayers for those who are not present and agree on who will follow up with them. The group may also express prayers for persons, leaders, and needs in the community and world.

Prayer of Thanksgiving

Each group reunion meeting ends with grateful awareness of the gifts that God has given us through one another and through the presence of the Holy Spirit as we go forth. The group may take a moment for individuals to name the gift they have received for the week to come. The group concludes with the "Prayer of Thanksgiving" and departs.

The Role of the Card

The role of the group reunion card is threefold:

① The card keeps the group focused and the sharing on track with a simple framework for the hour together. Sometimes special needs arise that require the group's attention. But as a rule, the card directs the flow of sharing in effective group reunions.

② The card guides the group in a spiritual conversation that flows from shallow waters to deeper waters in a natural way. Sharing moves from a review of individual commitments and practices into reflections on Christ's presence and call in the course of daily living.

③ The card links the group back to the message of the Emmaus weekend and forward to the vision of a life lived wholly in God's grace. The framework of the card represents the transforming partnership between Christians and Christ, combining attention to the discipline of growing discipleship with attention to the empowering presence of Christ in their lives.

As long as members' vision is growth toward a life in grace through the threefold discipline of discipleship, the reunion format will provide reinforcement and accountability to reach that goal.

Shared Leadership

Emmaus groups form around the principle of shared leadership. Every member of an Emmaus group is responsible for its leadership and its effectiveness for all. The group has no appointed leader and no officers. No one sends out notices about the meetings. Members do not depend on someone else to make the meeting meaningful. Rather, everybody is in charge of giving the best of themselves to God, to one another, and to the intent of the meeting. The common flow of the Emmaus group card guides the meeting. All members have a common desire that each person have time to share, and they support one another with prayerful respect as disciples of Jesus Christ.

In some groups, shared leadership is natural. The personalities and dynamics work together to allow meetings to flow smoothly. Members naturally assume responsibility for things that need doing to enable the meeting. In other groups, shared leadership means taking turns facilitating the meeting. Groups may rotate the facilitator role from week to week among the members of the group. The week's facilitator initiates the "Prayer to the Holy Spirit," leads off with each part of the card, sets the example in sharing, and generally moves the group through each transition to the closing "Prayer of Thanksgiving." ☦

How Can We Encourage Congregational Group Reunions?

obert Wood and Marie Livingston Roy write in *Day Four: The Pilgrim's Continued Journey*: "The sole purpose of the Emmaus Movement is to strengthen disciples within the ministry of individual congregations. . . . Emmaus does have a unique role in the life and ministry of the church in the church's task of nurturing strong committed disciples compassionately serving Christ in the world" (page 46).

Emmaus Potential in Congregations

Congregational and denominational leaders across the church have celebrated the potential and the actual results of the Walk to Emmaus in many churches as an agent of renewal for congregations. Individuals generally return to their churches with the fire of God's love rekindled within their hearts, with heightened commitment to Christ, and with expanded vision for the church as the body of Christ in mission. Especially in churches that nurture this personal renewal, the Emmaus experience commonly translates into outward effects such as:

✝ increased joy for the Lord;
✝ increased desire for vital worship and holy communion;
✝ increased willingness to serve, teach, and lead;
✝ increased hunger for Bible study and spiritual growth opportunities;
✝ increased financial giving;

- ✞ increased readiness to bear witness to Christ by sharing faith stories;
- ✞ increased vigor for mission and service;
- ✞ increased numbers of persons entering professional ministry.

Nurturing Group Reunions to Realize Potential

The most important way to realize the potential of the Emmaus experience in congregations is to nurture the formation of group reunions. The outcome of the Walk to Emmaus, at its best, is more than fired-up individuals. The fire within individuals, like coals in the fireplace, quickly loses its glow unless grouped for mutual support and exchange with others whose hearts are aflame. The optimal outcome of Emmaus is small communities of Christians within the body of Christ who keep one another close to the Source and who generate new life in the congregation through personal discipleship and leadership.

For this reason, Emmaus encourages every congregation to nurture group reunions as a follow-up to the Walk to Emmaus and encourages participants to make the group reunion a part of their lives. Because the Walk to Emmaus brings persons from many congregations together, group reunions often include persons from different churches. Whenever more than one person from the same church participates in Emmaus, the congregation should form group reunions.

Congregations can foster Emmaus group reunions in many ways:

Claim Emmaus group reunions as valuable parts of the congregation. Even though group reunions are generally self-initiated without oversight by church staff, they are no less a part of the congregation and its ministry. The congregation can foster the place of reunion groups in the nurturing ministry of the church by publicly affirming the steps of faith that the members have taken. Groups thrive when supported with space to meet, with leadership that appreciates their purpose, and with pastors who encourage them to mature and challenge them to serve.

Communicate openly about Emmaus and group reunions in the congregation. The greatest obstacle to the support of Emmaus groups in some congregations is an unfortunate air of secrecy and exclusivity that some associate with Emmaus. Persons should make every effort to eliminate this misunderstanding and to correct behaviors among participants in Emmaus that foster it. Open communication about the Walk to Emmaus and about active group reunions within the congregation through church newspapers and bulletin boards goes a long way toward dispelling myths. Make information about group reunions available throughout the congregation in the same way the church conveys other information about opportunities for growth as Christian disciples. Some churches refer to group reunions by other names (such as, accountability groups, discipleship groups, share groups, journey groups) in order to avoid the exclusive connotation in the word *reunion.*

Sponsor active members to grow as Christian disciples. Encourage sponsorship for the Emmaus weekend from within congregations but keep the purpose of Emmaus in mind when sponsoring. Then those who attend Emmaus generally return with readiness to continue their walk with Christ with other church members in group reunions and to share the gifts they are receiving with the congregation.

Emmaus exists for the deepening of discipleship and the strengthening of leaders among active church members. Emmaus is not a place to work through emotional problems, deal with grief, or evangelize non-Christians. Emmaus is not a tool for straightening out contentious members. Nor is it a movement for those persons who typically live on the theological fringe of the church.

When persons sponsor others without regard for the intent of the Emmaus program in the church, the effects in the church can be harmful. But when persons carry out sponsorship knowledgeably and on behalf of the church, groups of renewed and maturing members leaven the faith community as they come to celebrate and share what God has given, not just to receive what the church can give.

Incorporate new Emmaus participants into church groups as soon as possible. Congregational leaders actually have more motivation to nurture group reunions than Emmaus Community leaders because the potential payoff for the congregation is substantial and immediate. Some persons who participate in Emmaus will find groups among friends who are in other congregations. But when church members sponsor pilgrims from within the church, group reunions naturally form within the congregation.

When persons return from their Emmaus weekends, existing group reunions may invite them to join them or assist in the formation of new groups. In some churches, an Emmaus liaison person keeps an eye on those being sponsored, communicates with the pastor, and makes sure after their Walk that everybody finds a group. In other churches, persons who have returned from an Emmaus weekend receive an invitation to a gathering with other persons in the church who participated in Emmaus. They share experiences and form group reunions with the new participants.

Invite anyone who desires to grow as an accountable Christian. The three-day Emmaus experience provides the impetus for most persons to join a group reunion. But groups may include persons who have not been to the Walk to Emmaus. The heart of the group reunion is not the Emmaus experience, but a vision of a life lived wholly in the grace of God and a small-group covenant for living into that vision through the discipline of piety, study, and action. In a number of instances, persons' prior involvement in group reunions have led to their attending the Walk to Emmaus weekend.

Use Emmaus groups as part of the total program of Christian formation and spiritual growth. Emmaus groups represent one of several movements in the church today aimed at nurturing strongly committed Christians for service in the church and the world through an emphasis on accountable discipleship. In congregations, Emmaus group reunions can serve as one important avenue for adult Christian formation. Lay the foundation for these groups by having persons who desire to participate first attend the three-day Emmaus experience. Afterwards, persons form group reunions that continue in the life of the congregation, fostering Christian discipleship.

Various discipleship programs can complement one another and provide options for everyone. A congregation's exclusive encouragement of the Walk to Emmaus or any other single program as *the* pathway to spiritual growth will leave out many persons who cannot participate or who are not drawn to it.

Congregations can combine the Walk to Emmaus experience with a churchwide emphasis such as "Covenant Discipleship," which aims to recover the class meeting dynamic of the Wesleyan heritage. One congregation incorporated persons just off the Emmaus weekend into Covenant Discipleship groups in the church. Covenant Discipleship groups provide the same dynamics of accountability and sharing as the group reunion but without the perception of being limited to Emmaus participants. Some congregations have integrated the life review and accountability dynamic of the group reunion into existing Bible studies and prayer groups.

Give group members opportunities to dig deeper. Piety, study, and action do not come automatically as a life discipline, even in the afterglow of a wonderful Emmaus weekend. The Emmaus program does not offer ongoing education and nurture in these disciplines of the faith, which the congregation alone can offer. People return from the Walk to Emmaus motivated to develop a lifestyle of prayer and devotion, study and reflection, action and service. But they still need assistance in learning the art of daily prayer, getting into the Bible, and identifying their particular gifts for ministry.

One church invites persons following their Emmaus weekends to join a four- to six-week spiritual growth experience in small groups. The spiritual growth experience engages members in a guided course of daily prayer, meditation on scripture, and reflection on one's call to discipleship. Following the six weeks, the groups continue using the group reunion format. Another church encourages Emmaus participants to enter into a four-week experience to discover their gifts and call. Both churches prepare persons more fully for meaningful participation and continued growth through the weekly group reunion. ✞

How Can We Enhance Our Group Reunion's Effectiveness?

he group reunion may measure its effectiveness through each member's weekly success in walking with Christ, contributing to Christ's ministry through the church, and responding to Christ's call to serve in the everyday world. But group reunions often encounter difficulties along the way, which diminish their effectiveness as support bases for daily Christian discipleship and the quality of their community as a group. Enhancing the effectiveness of group reunions involves addressing the obstacles and seeking to nurture the quality of Christian community that groups enjoy.

Obstacles to Effective Group Reunions

Aimlessness is the plight of groups that lose their vision. They develop a comfortable weekly routine without challenge and without movement in grace on the part of the members. Though these groups think they are on the spiritual journey, in truth they have set up house along the way. They got to Emmaus, and they never left. Or they got off to a good start, but somewhere along the road, they lost their way and never seriously questioned what they were doing.

Aimless groups will rediscover their vitality as companions along the way as members reclaim and share their personal visions of the life of growth in the grace of Jesus Christ. They need to be honest with themselves and with God about the ways in which they may have let Emmaus, the group, or religion itself become a destination rather than a tent of meeting for pilgrims on a journey with Christ. Christ will lead them to new depths as they return to the beginning, revisit their commitments to God and one another, and reclaim a focus on the reunion card itself.

Anemia is the condition of groups that are losing their energy for the journey. They are made up of people who want to be on the journey but who doubt the group's ability to aid that process. The members lose their fervor and joy. Therefore, the value of getting to the meeting is less and less apparent. Members think highly of one another, but no one has time to continue to meet for the sake of meeting. Typically, some members leave the group without ever stating why for fear of hurting people's feelings.

Anemic groups regain their energy and reclaim their effectiveness by taking time apart to honestly assess members' concerns, hopes, and desires in relation to the group reunion. By admitting their feelings and addressing the problems together, groups sometimes realize that they can handle the source of their anemia. Perhaps some members are draining the group's lifeblood by their unconscious tendency to dominate the group with personal needs and conflicts, the insistence of a few to abandon the card, the wasting of group time in unrelated conversations, or the lack of seriousness on the part of some about their personal discipline. Renewal of the group awaits someone who will risk being vulnerable and who will call for openness about the group's future as an effective means of grace.

Superficiality may plague some groups. Each group functions at its own level of openness and self-disclosure. As group members journey together, they generally grow in knowledge of one another and therefore in their ability to support one another as pilgrims on the way. However, some groups do not grow in their knowledge and love of one another in ways that strengthen the group reunion as a support base for Christian living. Often the root of superficiality is fear of judgment, unwillingness to reveal imperfection, or distrust of certain individuals' discretion.

Some groups have moved through their superficiality by naming their impasse and addressing the fears that keep the sharing on the surface. Other groups simply have come to terms with the limitations of a one-hour weekly meeting to provide sufficient time for the sharing. They plan extended meetings on occasion or an annual day apart for more thorough exploration of life direction and goals for spiritual growth.

Isolationism may develop in some groups who isolate themselves within the church. They take a theological detour off of the mainstream path of the church marked by the breadth of orthodox Christian belief. Or they become self-righteous elitists who gain strength by feeling different, being critical, and setting themselves apart from the larger community of faith. Often, members of these groups are individuals who are angry at the church and are nursing hurt feelings. Unfortunately, the groups are effective in the wrong way. They enable one another to persevere in their unreconciled state and in their disruption to the church.

Such isolated groups need healing in order to regain their life as a true Emmaus group reunion and their fellowship with the larger church community. They need unconditional love and patience from the church community, which they themselves are presently unable to give. They also need the accountability of the church, which helps them to see what they have become. Church and Emmaus leaders must call such groups to be reconciled and to recover their effectiveness for building up the church in love.

Nurturing Christian Community in Group Reunions

The effectiveness of group reunions in supporting members' perseverance in grace as Christian disciples relates to the quality of Christian community nurtured among the participants. Group reunions are little Christian communities within the church and the larger community of faith. One helpful image of Christian community is that of a wagon wheel. The individual spokes of the wheel are the lives of people who connect in Christ, the hub. Like the spokes of a wheel, the closer we move toward Christ, the closer we come to one another as well.

Fostering a Sense of Christ's Presence

The wagon wheel image clearly illustrates how centering the meetings and relationships in Christ enhances the effectiveness of group reunions. One group cultivates a sense of Christ's presence by including an empty chair in its circle—a chair for the unseen Host of the meeting. This simple ritual serves as a constant reminder of the One who "came near and went with them" (Luke 24:15). The members conduct the meeting with heightened awareness of the presence of the Holy Spirit. Another group accomplishes the same purpose by placing a candle on a stand in the center of the group as a symbol of Christ's presence in their midst and in each person's heart.

By remaining centered in an awareness of Christ, the group reunion does not degenerate into a social club or just another meeting. Members are less inclined to minimize the value of the hour and waste the time in irrelevant conversation. The prayerful atmosphere fosters loving attentiveness to the voice of Christ through one another's sharing. Obstacles to the flow of love among groups members cry out to be dealt with respectfully and promptly in the healing and forgiving presence of Christ. The focus of the meeting remains on the walk with Christ, not on group dynamics or an effort to manufacture a sense of intimacy.

Showing Love for One Another

Prayer and sacrifice for one another also increase the effectiveness of group reunions. Some groups that suffer a sense of dryness might experience renewal by the waters of the Spirit through the simple practice of praying together. Sharing prayer with one another opens the floodgates of the heart to the free flow of God's love among the members. Groups can facilitate group prayer with simple methods such as those used on the Emmaus weekend. Pass a cross or Bible from person to person, asking each to offer a sentence prayer aloud or silently when receiving it.

Every Emmaus weekend is a reminder of the power of acts of agape and genuine sacrifice in expressing and fostering the love of

God among people. Sometimes groups weaken in spirit because nobody goes out of their way to make God's love visible. Simple acts of compassion, words of encouragement, or notes of support go a long way toward confirming the authenticity of group members' stated commitments to one another's spiritual welfare. Following up on missing members shows them they are remembered. Paying genuine attention to one another's stories and guarding the time for each to share are little acts of care that make the group a spiritual family.

Sharing a Common Resource in Prayer

Some group reunion members gain strength from one another and bond more tightly as a group by sharing a common prayer resource. For example, some groups make covenant to use the same devotional magazine or book to unite them in prayer day by day. The members then spend five minutes at the outset of the weekly meeting in prayerful reflection and sharing around the particular scripture or reading that most spoke to them that week. This focused sharing can help get the meeting off to a livelier start. *Alive Now* is an Upper Room publication, designed specifically to support the spiritual journeys of individuals in groups. Each issue offers a series of brief thematic readings and reflective questions.

Reminders for Effective Group Reunions

Commit yourselves, not only to God but to one another. Be regular in attendance and wholehearted in participation, not only for yourselves but on behalf of one another. When you least want to go to the meeting, another member may need the group most. When you feel you need it least is when you need it most.

Prepare yourselves ahead of time. Review the questions and your commitments before you arrive. Bring something to share. Remember each member in prayer; celebrate the grace in each one. Imagine Christ's going ahead to meet you there. Expect Christ to be there awaiting your arrival, prepared to hear you and to encourage you with a word you need to hear.

Practice your disciplines. Take the promises on the service sheet seriously—piety, study, and action. Remember that the greatest source of dullness in groups is members who do not practice the discipline during the week. If members have nothing to share and no practice to improve, then the group has no reason to meet. Group meetings do not make a person spiritual. The group cannot substitute for members' personal commitment to the discipline of life in grace. A group might occasionally take stock and ask, "Are we serious about the purpose of this group? Do we really want to live in grace through the practice of piety, study, and action?"

Be accountable to one another. Agree to be accountable to one another for your Christian practice and goals for growth. Do not let friends avoid the significance of their experience by giving superficial responses. Ask helpful questions; press for clarity. Remember one another's goals and plans for action. Inquire about one another's progress with the past week's plans; celebrate successes and forgive failures. Encourage the members of your reunion group. Be Christ for one another.

Uphold one another in prayer. Intercede for the members of your group regularly. Agree as a group to lift one another in prayer daily. Be there for one another in times of need. Share a common devotional resource to unite you in prayer throughout the week. Follow up when members are absent. When members move away, keep them with you in spirit and uphold them in love.

Focus on the group reunion card. Start with the service sheet and allow everyone to review his or her week. Then move on to the next section, asking everyone to respond to the questions. Use the whole card. If the time is short, focus on particular questions for deeper sharing, accountability, and avoidance of superficiality. Honor the order but do not be afraid to make adjustments to meet the needs of the group. Foster a sense of the Holy Spirit's leadership but allow time for each person. Encourage each member to participate at his or her own level and to respond to one another's needs.

Retreat with one another. Go apart as a group for a quiet day once each year for spiritual conversation, reflection on scripture, and prayer. Make this day a time to share life goals, review commitments, and identify needs for growth. This day apart will deepen the value of the mutual support and accountability in the weekly meetings.

Plan your discipleship. The group reunion supports a life of growth in grace undergirded by the personal discipline of piety, study, and action. Set personal goals with regard to your Christian devotion and discipleship. Share and test your goals with one another. Do not skip "Your Plan" for the week to come. Pray for one another's perseverance.

Act as a group in mission. Make a specific plan to be in mission as a group—in your church, in the Emmaus community, or in your local community. This working together deepens the bonds and the sense of companionship as Christians. Acting together encourages and inspires Christian action on the part of members. It also keeps the group from becoming an end in itself.

Be spiritual friends. Help one another be faithful to what is best within himself or herself. Keep the fire of God's love burning within one another. Deal with specific needs and challenges in one another's lives. Don't just "do" the card. Confirm what is deepest and most true in one another's hearts. Avoid self-righteous expectations and judgments; be real and human with one another.

Focus on the present, not analysis of the past. Avoid becoming an amateur group therapy session. Guard against the desire to "fix" one another and to solve one another's problems. Leave psychoanalysis to professional psychologists. Know when to guide friends to their pastors and to counselors.

Remember who you are in humility. Avoid becoming a group of self-righteous pharisees. Being in a group reunion does not make anyone better or more pleasing in God's eyes than others. It is less a sign of virtue as of one's acknowledgment of spiritual need for God and for the support of others.

Be open but low-key about the group. Avoid becoming a clique. Jesus instructed his disciples to pray but in a closet; to fast but without making a public display of it. Handle membership in group reunions in the same low-key manner. Always convey openness to others who hunger for what the group reunion represents. ☦

Resources

Emmaus Library Series

What Is Emmaus? by Stephen D. Bryant ~ Answers frequently asked questions about Emmaus, the Emmaus community, and follow-up groups. #41

The Group Reunion by Stephen D. Bryant ~ For persons who have participated in the Walk to Emmaus, guidance on the purpose and practice of the group reunion. #42

The Board of Directors by Richard A. Gilmore ~ Responsibilities and duties of the board committees, possible committee assignments, and more. #67E

Spiritual Directors by Kay Gray ~ Addresses the role of spiritual directors: qualifications; responsibilities before, during, and after the event. #68

Spiritual Growth through Team Experience by Joanne Bultemeier ~ A companion piece for the *Team Manual* and *Sustaining the Spirit*. Explains qualities of a team member, spiritual benefits of team membership, what happens at team meetings, and leadership development. #69

Coming Down from the Mountain: *Returning to Your Congregation* by Lawrence Martin ~ To help pilgrims make the transition back to their congregations, this booklet includes fun and informative chapters such as Long-Term Obedience in a Single Direction, Agape Unplugged, and On Not Being an Emmaus Groupie. #70

Walking Side by Side: *Devotions for Pilgrims* by Joanne Bultemeier and Cherie Jones ~ Forty-five meditations based on the fifteen talks given during The Walk offer a way to continue disciplines of prayer and meditation. #73

Sponsorship by Richard and Janine Gilmore ~ A guide through the process of sponsoring fellow pilgrims. Explores the range of possibilities in the role of the sponsor for the renewal of church leaders, Emmaus communities, and the church. #873

Music Directors by Sandy Stickney ~ Practical insights on topics ranging from ego to copyright requirements. Written with humor, directness, and a spirit of servanthood. #911

Additional resources for your journey toward piety, study, and action:
PIETY
Beginning Prayer by John Killinger, #676
A Book of Personal Prayer: Compiled by René Bideaux, #812
Calming the Restless Spirit: *A Journey toward God* by Ben
 Campbell Johnson, #814
Devotional Life in the Wesleyan Tradition by Steve Harper, #467

Dimensions of Prayer: *Cultivating a Relationship with God* by Douglas V. Steere, #800

A Guide to Prayer for Ministers and Other Servants, #559

A Guide to Prayer for All God's People by Norman Shawchuck and Rueben P. Job, #710

Heartfelt: *Finding Our Way Back to God* by Gerrit Scott Dawson, #684

Invitation to Presence: *A Guide to Spiritual Disciplines* by Wendy Miller, #736

Journaling: *A Spiritual Journey* by Anne Broyles, #866

Journeying Through the Days: *A Calendar & Journal for Personal Reflection*, annual

Praying through the Lord's Prayer by Steve Harper, #656

Sending Up My Timber: *An African American Prayer Journal* by Karen F. Williams and Lloyd Preston Terrell, #856

The Upper Room Disciplines: *A Book of Daily Devotions,* annual

Winter Grace: *Spirituality and Aging* by Kathleen Fischer, #850

STUDY

An Adventure in Healing and Wholeness: *The Healing Ministry of Christ in the Church Today* by James K. Wagner, #689

Alone with God: *A Guide for Personal Retreats* by Ron DelBene with Mary and Herb Montgomery, #668

As If the Heart Mattered: *A Wesleyan Spirituality* by Gregory S. Clapper, #820

The Breath of Life: *A Workbook, A Simple Way to Pray* by Ron DelBene with Mary and Herb Montgomery #766

Called by a New Name: *Becoming What God Has Promised* by Gerrit Scott Dawson, #802

Discovering Community: *A Meditation on Community in Christ* by Stephen Doughty, #870

Forming Faith in a Hurricane: *A Spiritual Primer for Daily Living* by N. Graham Standish, #848

Heart Whispers: *Benedictine Wisdom for Today* by Elizabeth J. Canham, #892

Journeymen: *A Spiritual Guide for Men (And Women Who Want to Understand Them)* by Kent Ira Groff, #862

Neglected Voices: *Biblical Spirituality in the Margins* by John Indermark, #891

Reading with Deeper Eyes: *The Love of Literature and the Life of Faith* by William H. Willimon, #847

Remember Who You Are: *Baptism, a Model for Christian Life* by William H. Willimon, #399

Remembering Your Story: *A Guide to Spiritual Autobiography* by Richard L. Morgan, #781

Responding to God: *A Guide to Daily Prayer* by Martha Graybeal Rowlett, #783

Shaped by the Word: *The Power of Scripture in Spiritual Formation* by M. Robert Mulholland Jr., #519

Sunday Dinner: *The Lord's Supper and the Christian Life* by William H. Willimon, #429

The Upper Room Spiritual Classics, Series 1 Compiled and introduced by Keith Beasley-Topliffe, #832

The Upper Room Spiritual Classics, Series 2 Compiled and introduced by Keith Beasley-Topliffe, #853

The Upper Room Spiritual Classics, Series 3 Compiled and introduced by Keith Beasley-Topliffe, #905

The Workbook of Intercessory Prayer by Maxie Dunnam, #382

The Workbook of Living Prayer by Maxie Dunnam, #718

The Workbook on Becoming Alive in Christ by Maxie Dunnam, #542

The Workbook on Spiritual Disciplines by Maxie Dunnam #479

The Workbook on the Christian Walk by Maxie Dunnam #640

The Workbook on Virtues & the Fruit of the Spirit by Maxie Dunnam and Kimberly Dunnam Reisman, #854

Writing on the Heart: *Inviting Scripture to Shape Daily Life* by Gerrit Scott Dawson, #713

ACTION

And Not One Bird Stopped Singing: *Coping with Transition and Loss in Aging* by Doris Moreland Jones, #815

Children and Prayer: *A Shared Pilgrimage* by Betty Shannon Cloyd, #803

Discovering Grace in Grief by James L. Mayfield, #696

Finding a Spiritual Friend *How Friends and Mentors Can Make Your Faith Grow* by Timothy Jones, #857

The Godbearing Life: *The Art of Soul Tending for Youth Ministry* by

Kenda Creasy Dean and Ron Foster, #858

Growing Together in Love: *God Known through Family Life* by Anne Broyles, #687

Heart of Healing, Heart of Light: *Encountering God Who Shares Our Pain* by Flora Slosson Wuellner, #666

In the Shadow of God's Wings: *Grace in the Midst of Depression* by Susan Gregg-Schroeder, #807 (Leader's Guide also available #859)

Into the Light: *A Simple Way to Pray with the Sick and the Dying* by Ron DelBene, #576

Near Life's End: *What Family and Friends Can Do* by Ron DelBene with Mary and Herb Montgomery, #578

Prayer, Stress and Our Inner Wounds by Flora Slosson Wuellner, #501

Rediscovering Our Spiritual Gifts: *Building up the Body of Christ through the Gifts of the Spirit* by Charles V. Bryant, #633

Sacramental Living: *Falling Stars and Coloring Outside the Lines* by Dwight and Linda Vogel, #889

Then Shall Your Light Rise: *Spiritual Formation and Social Witness* by Joyce Hollyday, #816

To Heal the Earth: *A Theology of Ecology* by Frederick Quinn, #702

Transforming Ventures: *A Spiritual Guide for Volunteers in Mission* by Jane Ives, #910

Yours Are the Hands of Christ by James C. Howell, #867

Emmaus publications are available only from The Upper Room®:
Walk to Emmaus (formerly Pilgrim's Guide #1)
Lay Director's Manual (#4)
Spiritual Director's Manual (#7)
Lay Talk Outlines (#11)
Clergy Talk Outlines (#12)
Kitchen Manual (#15)
Walk to Emmaus (Spanish Edition, #20)
Day Four (#553)

TO ORDER CALL 1 (800) 972-0433.
Except for those noted, resources are also available through your Cokesbury bookstore.